We Will Eat Break
With Our Childr

Niall M. Oliver

Published by Nine Pens Press

2023

www.ninepens.co.uk

ISBN: 978-1-7391517-6-8

021

5   Grandmother's Winter

6   Early Onset

7   Blue Grandad

9   He Who Travels Has Stories To Tell

10 Just Like On TV

11 I Want To Tell You Something To Remember

12 Her Prayer Book Was Frayed And Held Together With String

14 I Could Eat You Up

15 Moses Basket 3:26am

16 Diminished Responsibility

17 A Tyre Changer Can Earn £350k Per Year

18 Grateful For Very Tiny Ladybirds

19 Do You Come Here Often?

20 The Summer You Went Away To Washington

21 Weekend In Paris

22 We'd Lived Here For Seven Years

23 A New Season

24 Hourglass

25 The Groundsman

26 Reflection

27 Some Dad Moments

28 Questions From A Five Year Old

29 In My Olden Days

30 Child Soldiers

31 A Boy I Used To Know

32 Summer Job

33 Magic At The Morning Market

34 Tactics

35 Smoking Fingers

36 My Brother And I Were Never Closer

37 Adrian

38 Recurring

Grandmother's Winter

As if searching for a key in the dark
she fumbles around in her mind
for my name, but like chimney smoke
it has drifted away again. Instead,
from a pocket of her winter coat
she pulls out two lumps of coal,
strays gathered on the stroll home
past Grahams' fuel yard. I say nothing
as she places them carefully among
the embers of the fire, and watch
as she blows black dust from her fingers,
before hitching up her skirt hem,
just enough to warm the backs of her legs.
I see no point in reminding her again
that the old cast iron fireplace is now
an electric faux coal & flame effect,
and then like a door snib that's just been released,
she snaps, *For Christ's sake Niall,*
don't just sit there, go and fill the scuttle!

Early Onset

Startled from my teenage dreams,
I see a stooped spectre
hovering at the foot of my bed.

A luminous gown hangs
from the nightwalker's frame
like the sag of a denture-less jaw.

Even my footballing heroes
battling silently on the walls
appear spooked;

some with eyes agog,
others grimace and can barely look
as the white-haired ghoul

unsure of which world it is in,
turns to face me. Our eyes meet
and I recognise her stare,

not deathly, but confused.
I take her hand, not cold,
but warm and fragile,

like that of a child.

Blue Grandad

We called him Blue Grandad, not because his eyes were milky blue like larimars, or because he always wore blue overalls, but because he only ever drove blue cars. He said the colour *blue* reminded him of the ocean where he'd sailed for months at a time as an engineer on merchant navy ships. *I was only there in case we got a flat wheel,* was his usual joke. When he wasn't making us laugh, he was reciting the poems he'd written in the quiet of his dimly lit bunk. Dipping his pen into the water's black well, he'd tell of the brightest stars he'd ever seen; stars which the sky would surrender to the sea, only for them to taunt the waves by rising again. There was a poem about a pâtissier from Aquitaine who could plait pastry quicker than he could tie his boots, and one about a fortune teller who wore a trail of jewels across the smooth golden sands of her belly. He also wrote about home and the things he missed; cutting turf at Mackle's bog, the walk to chapel on Sundays, the funeral of his youngest brother.

One time when reading me a poem about fishing for eels at dawn in Lough Neagh, he stopped midway, and looked up beyond me, as if he'd heard something in the distance. I watched his lips silently shape a word. Then he leaned in, and beckoned me over with his hand, and whispered, *I was ordered up one night, you know, up on deck, to give the men a hand. There was trouble. I'd fired a gun before, but…*then he leaned even closer, the bows of our faces almost touching. *I maybe killed a man or two that night.* And for once, silence filled the space between us, like a long em dash. And from each end, we clung, drifting there together for what seemed a nautical mile, until finally, with a sparkle of larimar and a wink of an eye, it broke. Then he straightened himself, and after a long intake of breath, cast us off again into the early morning mist.

He Who Travels Has Stories To Tell

My mother was busy questioning
        her faith,
as I folded my wardrobe
         into a case.

Summer in The States, *my* prayers
         answered,
digs in the Bronx and flights
         sponsored.

She bids me to stay safe, slips a purse
         in my pocket,
inside, a relic of my namesake
         St. Oliver Plunkett;

a blessed fragment of bone. She tells me:
         ring home often,
find a chapel, don't be out
         on your lonesome,

remember that young lad who came home
         in a hearse,
and for God's sake, son,
         don't lose that purse.

Just Like On TV

At the airport, my host held up a cardboard sign
with my name, and drove me to a 24hr diner
in an air-conditioned, automatic sedan.
The waitress there asked how I'd like my eggs.
Yellow taxis zig-zigged along the freeway
as we crossed the east river towards the Bronx.
In the distance, Manhattan was fluorescent,
each tower bigger and brighter than the next.
There was a chalk drawing of a body
on the pavement near my apartment block.
My stomach lurched at the scent of a skunk
as gangs loitered at each end of the street.
A cockroach raced around the elevator floor.
I called my parents to say I'd arrived
and told them it was even better than I'd imagined.
The telephone cord was at least six metres long.

I Want To Tell You Something To Remember

The last I'd heard before boarding at JFK
was that you were waiting for me,
and when I arrived in Dublin at day break
my brother told me you didn't make it
through the night. I don't recall much after that,
like who cried and who didn't, and did I?
If not for the gold leaf lettering
on your gravestone; the date of your dying,
I swear I would have forgotten that too.

People tell me how well you looked, lying
in your coffin, *just like herself,* they say.
Did it rain as we carried you to the church?
But I did carry you, an undeniable fact,
though my body bears no memory of your weight.
Yet the swing and clang of your garden gate
still rings fresh in my mind, when I called to say goodbye,
two months earlier, a short stay, a big boy in a rush,
eager to get away.

I drank half a cup of tea as you cleared ashes
from the hearth. Every visible speck swept,
the soft scraping of shovel on stone,
and before a match was struck I was gone.
I wish I'd held you longer, or told you
something to remember, as you stood
at your doorstep, watching me walk away.

Her Prayer Book Was Frayed And Held Together With String

I was always first in line for a treat
from Granny's purse. A bag of sweets
or a few coins for my money box.
If I was misbehaving or being bold
she'd wave at me with the sally rod,
but never use it. I was her favourite.
My brother and cousins never stood a chance.
After Grandad passed, I stayed with her at night.
We'd chat and play hands of whist or rummy.
Before bed, she'd insist we kneel for the rosary,
then boil up a sip of milk in the pan to help us sleep,
and a hot water bottle for her feet.
I was twenty-seven when she died.
We hadn't talked properly in years,
Alzheimer's jumbled the words in her mouth and ears.
But as soon as she was gone I believed
she could hear me again. I'd talk to her,
tell her things about my life.
One time I faced a problem I couldn't figure by myself
and asked for her help. I wept as I spoke,
told her how much I missed her,
had been missing her for many years.
At that moment, amidst my prayers and tears,
a 'Thank You' card someone had given me
tumbled from the chest of drawers in my room
and landed upright on the floor by my feet.

Sometime later I relayed this story to a priest.
He wondered if I'd brushed the card with my arm
on the way past, or perhaps a window was open
and maybe there was a draught?
I asked Granny what she'd make of faith like that.

I Could Eat You Up

I absolutely could! says your Grandmother,
as she shares you around like a birthday cake.
She claims your *elegant fingers* for herself,
then serves your *sturdy farmer's legs* to Grandad.
Beaming Aunties are dished your *perfect smile*,
whilst your eyes go to your Mum, just as they did
that first moment you lay glazed and sticky on her skin.
For me? Not as much as a toe, so I wait patiently
until everyone goes, then piece you back together,
smoothing your joins with my lips. I place
your ear to my heart, and whisper you to rest,
as you send out puff after puff of buttercream breath —
my generous boy, still giving in your sleep.

Moses Basket 3.26am

As I lay him down gently
silk skin lightly glistening
I imagine I'm a ninja
and him nitro-glycerine.

Diminished Responsibility

So, you are saying, when your son is sleeping
his legs bunch up by his sides
like those on a roast chicken,
and when you hold him to your cheek
the hairs on his head prickle like a kiwi fruit?
Furthermore, his skin has a hint of strawberry,
and his chin is always dripping wet
as if glazed in a coat of honey?

That's correct. I would also like to add
that his little toes have even begun
to smell of camembert cheese.

And these are the reasons you felt compelled
to tell him that you could eat him up?

Yes, I'm afraid so.

And when you carried him to the kitchen,
did the boy cry out?

Yes, Your Honour, he did, tenderly
like a spring lamb.

A Tyre Changer Can Earn £350k Per Year

When I look back, I picture a multi-million pound
Formula One pit crew,
making snap decisions at break-neck speed,
but instead of shaving seconds off,
this team's goal is to add precious time
onto precious lives —

underpaid NHS nurses
and midwives rush around the motionless bodies
of my wife and new-born child,
their engines barely ticking over,
me, an open-mouthed spectator,

but today there will be no final lap
or chequered flag, as light reappears
in my wife's eyes, and our son's first cries
fill the room. Our race goes on,
and just like that our pit-crew has gone,

leaving us to cheer upon our podium,
with rounds of buttery toast and hot cups of tea.

Grateful For Very Tiny Ladybirds

On Friday and Saturday nights
in villages, towns and cities everywhere,
girls and boys make their way to clubs and bars,
styled up in their coolest gear,
lipstick and aftershave from ear-to-ear,
shiny dresses and their best checked-shirts,
and soon they're checking one another out,
and dancing, drinking, laughing and singing,
but most of all they come for the kissing.

They kiss people they like the look of.
They kiss people they've never met before.
They kiss people whose names they don't know.
They kiss their friends and their friends' friends
and then they start all over again.
But every now and then, although it is very rare,
for one of these kissers
an unexpected and unusual event may occur:

a very tiny ladybird no bigger than a speck of sugar
leaps mid-kiss from the tongue of one of the kissers,
and makes its way very quickly towards
the emotional centre of the other kisser's brain,
where it plants a tiny heart-shaped flag,
and from that exact moment, that person
will never desire to kiss another human being,
apart from the one they are kissing,
and they'll be very happy about that —
I'm very happy about that.

Do You Come Here Often?

Your mother warned you to never trust a salesman.
She said, "their eyes are always dancing",
which had me on the back foot from the start,
even though I swore I was useless at it, *selling–*

and to prove it, I rang my boss to back me up.
He didn't answer any of my calls, before
or after I left the pub, but the next morning
having listened to my lengthy voicemails,

summoned me to his office and confirmed,
I was neither hunter nor gatherer; weak
at closing, and always letting good leads
slip away. I wondered then what you'd say.

If only I'd asked for your number.

The Summer You Went Away To Washington

Every time I looked at the sky, it was as grey
as every picture of Abraham Lincoln I'd ever seen,
and the rain streamed incessantly down my window panes.

This isn't a metaphor to explain
how I was feeling without you —
it really did just piss down the whole summer,

and I felt like crying every day.

Weekend In Paris

I'd hoped the cruise on the Seine would be the highlight,
but it wasn't. Nor was the open top bus tour.
We inched up the Eiffel Tower as if climbing Mont Blanc.
It was February 2012, and Europe was in the grip
of a freak cold wave. Paris froze still as a gargoyle.

There was that romantic meal in Montmartre,
at a seafood brasserie with views across the city,
but that wasn't the highlight either.
The most memorable moment came when we returned
to our hotel room:

I hurriedly took off my trousers
and joined my wife on the rim of the ensuite bath,
where we sat and paddled our feet in lukewarm water,
giddy as toddlers in a rockpool.
Come bedtime we were puking up oysters.

We'd Lived Here For Seven Years

The day we left London for good,
I met a man who lives at the bottom of our street.
He commented on how many belongings
we had packed into the removal truck.

He also mentioned how polluted the air here
had become with traffic fumes.
But overall he concluded it was a lovely neighbourhood,
that the people in this street were particularly welcoming.

He wished me luck and shook my hand,
and as he walked away he told me his name was Mike.
He said, *I hope you like it here,*
I'm sure I'll see you around.

A New Season

My father ambles along the garden path,
the image of a man half his age.

With the warmth of spring on his side,
and in no rush whatsoever, he gently wheels

a stroller with his grandson asleep inside.
It's been a while since he pushed one of those,

I say to my mother, who replies, *Maybe never —*
you see, men didn't do that kind of thing in his day.

And I think to myself, what an awful pity,
because it really does suit him,

that kind of thing.

Hourglass

The sight of the tall firs, like guards at the gateway,
cue our boys to shout, *We're here already!*
The drone of car wheels softens where the tarry
road lightens, blending seamlessly into the sandy
seven-mile stretch; a lopsided smile, arching all the way
east to Downhill beach. Sea and sky wear matching grey,
each, randomly specked with white foam and stray
gulls, freezing like kites in the headwind. *Hurry, hurry,*
come calls from the back, as doors fly open, and away
they rush as if sucked out by a tsunami pull, willingly.
We marvel at their wildness, aware of our opportunity
to sail along on their coattails, to let the wind carry
their smiles onto our faces, knowing that eventually
the sand will shift beneath their feet — but not today.

The Groundsman

I wake at a quarter to five
to a single cry from the baby.
A nightmare maybe,
perhaps scared his endless milk supply
might actually end. Or that today
he'll be kissed less than yesterday.

That one, brief, exotic-sounding shriek,
enough to yank the pull-cord of my mind,
forcing my engine into action,
propelling its worn blade round and round
in familiar circles.
He's gone back to sleep, lucky bundle.

I push further into the jungle.

Reflection

In the six or seven minutes
it takes for the oats to soak
and thicken to a cream, I find
myself staring at the sweet spot,

the moment in-between, when night
hands-over to morning's light: a robin
hopping along the garden fence,
a distant tree crowned with starlings,

pearls of water gleaming
on the surely greening grass,
and the silvery sheen of the lough,
with just a hint of mist atop,

all slowly becoming clear,
as the man in my pyjamas
looks back at me and stirs,
until he disappears.

Some Dad Moments

There's no talking to our youngest
as he pulls at my finger,
tugging us to the cupboard
where the red biscuit tin stays.
His target locked,
his little head nodding,
we both know he isn't asking.

Our first-born loves bedtime stories,
dinosaur books make him roar,
ONE MORE! ONE MORE!
So, after three more,
I kiss him goodnight
and he teases, *I'll wipe it away!*
With a swish of a raptor's tail, it's gone.

When our house finally rests,
my wife and I draw breath,
inhaling nostalgic aromas
from grapes in our glasses.
I recognise a look in her eyes
as she promises, *We'll do all those couple things*
again one day darling…but,

wouldn't it be nice to have a girl too?
I sigh. The clock ticks.

Questions From A Five Year Old

They come as fast as NERF gun darts:
what, when, where, why, why and more why.
Tonight my son wants to know when I am going to die.
He asks me what age he will be when it happens.
He asks what age I will be.
I tell him that I don't know when I will die.
But I reassure him that I am healthy and well,
that it won't happen for a very long time.
I remind him that I am only forty-four years old.
Forty-four years old is very old he says.
He asks me what life was like in the olden days.

In My Olden Days

There was no iPlayer,
no Google or WhatsApp
or YouTube or podcasts,
no inkling of a World Wide Web,
so instead, at 6pm every day

during Northern Ireland's troubled eighties,
parents from both communities
in every house on every street
would unite, turn to their children,
and in harmony, shout:

Whist weans, the news is on!

Child Soldiers

A nation? says Bloom. A nation is the same people living in the same place.

                                     -     *Ulysses*

There is an invisible dividing wall
which runs along the gangway of the school bus.
It is decades old, built from blocks of history,
cemented with blood and spit.
In case the wall should falter, the trade
is passed on, brother to brother, like nits.
The soldiers step aboard in single file,
graffiti flags wave them to their seats.

A fenian spy *accidentally* drops his books at his feet,
cups his ear as he stoops to pick them up,
then returns to base with news of a protestant plot
to blow up the science teacher with a whoopee cushion.
He heard them vote *Shoot* as their favourite magazine,
says they swore blind that St Mary's girls are dynamite
compared to the prudish girls at their school.
The spy concludes:

Them prods are just like us!

A Boy I Used To Know

I don't tell my new friends about the boy
who'd blow his pocket-money on rolls
of caps to make 2p bangers,

then at dark-fall, launch them like grenades
against the wall of his protestant neighbours' house,
driving them mad, driving them out.

I don't tell them of the names he'd mutter
at the soldiers patrolling check-points and streets,
or the freedom songs he'd sing with his mates.

I don't tell how the boy would feel the impact
somewhat less, when the news of another death
bore the name of a victim from the other side.

I'm too afraid they wouldn't understand
if I spoke of this boy, and how he'd revolt
at the sound of their English tongues.

Summer Job

Tuesdays and Fridays are my favourite days.
My father and I sail along the north west coast
in a blue and white box-lorry, where all the town-
names begin with *Port,* and where people wear t-shirts
and shorts, even in the rain.

The shops here sell souvenirs by the bucketful,
and ice cream in spades. Neon signs blink
in letters large enough for Finn McCool to read.
We call at grocery stores and supermarkets
to replenish their fruit and vegetable stocks.

My father slips his pen out from behind his ear,
opens his duplicate book, makes a list: apples,
potatoes, tomatoes, lettuce, bananas, grapes.
After we carry in the boxes and crates, I listen
to my father and the shop owner chat like old friends.

Then off we go again, always making good time
for the next stop. At clockwork intervals
my father reminds me about the importance
of my education: *Son,*
you don't want to end up working a job like this.

He has to say it firmly, on Tuesdays and Fridays.

Magic At The Morning Market

He appears to choose at random,
my dad, reaching into the basket
with his finger and thumb
to reveal a single red apple.
He places it on his open palm,

and holds it out for us to look,
as if a crystal ball that any second
might levitate. *Sweet as a bell in a wood,*
he says, before tossing for the grocer to catch,
and through the air, it sparkles.

Tactics

A hedgerow runs the length of our garden.
On the other side is the primary school's grass pitch.
Mum thinks the hedge isn't tall enough. Dad says
one of these days he'll build a wall in its place.

Some evenings, big boys from the village play football
on the pitch. I watch through gaps in the hedge.
One team always takes their tops off, even when it's raining.
They shout a lot and thud into each other like dodgems.

When it gets dark they smoke cigarettes and get so loud
I can hear them from inside. Sometimes there are sounds
like bottles smashing. Today, I see my dad through a gap.
He is talking to the boys. One of them walks towards him.

Mum whisks me away from the hedge.
When Dad comes in I'm bristling with questions.
He says they were just discussing tactics.
I ask him what tactics are. I ask him what a *fucker* is.

Smoking Fingers

Before Sunday dinner,
my brother scrubs hard the yellow

from his two smoking fingers
until they blush like mortified teenagers

who scream, *don't look at us!*

My Brother And I Were Never Closer

Than the Christmas morning beneath the tree,
shoulder to shoulder, unwrapping pairs
of red boxing gloves left by a naive Santa.
After one brutal round we remained in our corners.

We lived in different worlds in the same house.
His had blinds drawn and smelled of nicotine.
He played its anthem in heavy metal.
Earrings and Doc Martens were mandatory.

In my territory, walls were made from mirrors.
Intruders were warned off by badly sung ballads
and clinking of dumbbells. Sports trophies doubled
as cudgels. Parents would patrol the hallway in riot gear.

Nowadays we are softer in the middle, wives and kids
carry olive branches. We check in every so often,
a quick *hi* and *how's tricks?* Last time around
we agreed Coldplay aren't bad.

Knowing we are as close as we'll ever be,
we've found contentment in this new place,
inhabiting the space we never could —
just a screen-swipe away, in each other's pockets.

Adrian

You have a warm smile
You are twenty-six years old
You are strawberry blonde like your siblings
You have strong shoulders and a six-pack to envy
You are captain of the football team
You have presence, yet are modest and shy
You make people laugh
You have many friends — I am one of them
You have a wife who loves you
Your parents are quietly proud of you
You have a little brother who idolises you
You are a skilled carpenter
You have calloused hands
You built a beautiful home with them
You are especially pleased with the oak staircase
You hope to have children one day
You would be a good dad
You deserve to be happy
You don't deserve to have this cancer
You can beat it
You die within weeks of the diagnosis
You never stood a chance
You gave everything in your short life
You've been gone for seventeen years
You are so badly missed
You appear in my dreams again
You have a warm smile

Recurring

1)
I've lost count of the times I've walked
out those doors and down those steps,
clutching the same slip of paper in my hand.
Sometimes I fold it in half and it doubles in size.
Sometimes I'm wearing it like a sandwich board.
Often the steps transform into a slide.
All around are the faces of fellow pupils
who celebrate in packs. When they hug
I gasp for breath. Each high five stings my cheek.
Their slips fill the air like ticker tape.
I walk fast and keep my gaze to the ground,
avoiding eye contact in case anyone would ask.
I haven't looked at the paper
but I already know what it says:

You Have Fucked Your Life Up Big Time

2)
I am awake now. There is no slip of paper in my hand.
All is quiet. I wrap the quiet around myself like a blanket.
Beside me, my wife lies still and warm.
I allow myself to rest in the rhythmic tide of her breath.
In a few hours we will get up, wash and dress.
We will eat breakfast with our children.

Acknowledgments

My thanks to my wife and sons for their love and support, as well as providing me with endless inspiration.

My gratitude to all my writer friends from across the globe who have read and commented on these poems, especially those at SC.

Thanks also go to the editors of publications where some of these poems, or earlier versions of them were published: *Acumen, The Honest Ulsterman, Atrium, Fly On The Wall Press, Poets Directory, Alchemy Spoon, The Madrigal, and others.*

Finally, I would like to thank Colin Bancroft, editor of Nine Pens Press, for believing in my work.

9 781739 151768